Out of Darkness

Out of Darkness

A Poetic Journey through Trauma

HANNAH BATTISTE

OUT OF DARKNESS
A POETIC JOURNEY THROUGH TRAUMA

This publication was made possible with funding from:
McGill University

More than Words Research Program

Everfair Research & Evaluation Consulting

Everfair
Research & Evaluation
Consulting

iUniverse books may be ordered through booksellers or by contacting:

iUniverse
1663 Liberty Drive
Bloomington, IN 47403
www.iuniverse.com
844-349-9409

ISBN: 978-1-6632-4407-9 (sc)
ISBN: 978-1-6632-4406-2 (e)

Library of Congress Control Number: 2022915265

Print information available on the last page.

iUniverse rev. date: 09/28/2022

Contents

Trigger Warning ix

Preface xi

Part One: Tragedies that Became Meaning 1

    Betrayal 3

    Little Teenaged Girl 5

    Her 8

    The Way Out 10

    Images 12

    Times 13

    Knowing 14

    Darkness 16

    Suffering 17

    Feelings 18

Part Two: Inspirations 19

    Brother 21

    Friend 22

    Females 23

    Conflicted 25

    Journey 27

    Mirrors 28

    Human 29

    Our People 31

    Warriors 33

Reminder 35

No Goodbyes 36

Belief.. 38

Part Three: Finding Myself **39**

Beginnings 41

Disguise 43

Confident 45

Tongue-Tied 46

The Fade.. 47

Forgiveness.. 49

Finding My Way 51

Calling... 53

I Am the Reason 54

Making it 55

Afterword... 57

Writing and Drawing Prompts 59

For Rita Joe

Trigger Warning

This book contains sensitive material that includes but is not necessarily limited to

- bullying
- sexual assault
- self-harm
- trauma
- racism
- grief
- mental Illness
- suicidal intent

Preface

This book was compiled from poems I wrote over the last eight years. I have revised many of them, but they still reflect where I was at the time of writing and the way I experienced the things happening to me then. Gathering them for this book has taken me on an eye-opening journey.

Writing this book was like trying to climb a big lighthouse. I was often afraid, I was often stuck, and I often felt so tired I didn't know if I could go on. But I continued my journey. I found the answers I have been looking for: I found myself, I found relief, and I found acceptance. I was inspired. Writing this book felt as though I was working on someone else's story, but it was my own.

As I reread everything, I started to put the puzzle pieces together. It seemed that for years I had been putting the pieces in the wrong places. Often these wrong places did not have to do with me, but I accepted that I was where I had to be in order to get to where I am now. I was never fully put together, and I was missing some things.

I used to think my work was going to result in nothing; no one was going to read it, and no one was going to care. But someone finally noticed me. As I reread every poem, drew the images, and put everything together, I was put back into those moments when I was writing those poems, with all the tears and memories splashed onto the walls. I was afraid the whole time; I was afraid to express myself and afraid to be heard. It was like I had to block some of myself out, but then I remembered that this is my story, this is my life, and this is how I want to inspire people. I must be myself.

I explain my life and my mental illness as being like a lighthouse: I started at the bottom, and I built my way up to the top where all the light was. But every time something happened, I was knocked down to the bottom, afraid in the darkness, trying to find my way back up. I knew exactly what to do and where to go each time, but I still felt stuck. It took a lot of me to build myself back up again, but I did it, and I realized that all those times I thought I needed to find the light, the light had always been me.

I thought I needed to have this big breakthrough moment, when all along I had it inside myself. It takes a lot to look at yourself and to see bravery, strength, resilience, faith, and love. You spend your life wondering if everything would be easier if you just offed yourself, but then you realize that so much more pain and darkness comes from that. I still have those dark days, but I know now that I am the light out of darkness.

Take a deep breath for my journey:
one, two, three …
breathe …

PART ONE

Tragedies that Became Meaning

Bad things happen to everyone, and most times they are out of our control. Some of the things that happened in my life were unexpected. In my mind, I needed control because I was never able to control what happened to me and what went on inside my brain. I felt useless, and I felt as though everything was my fault.

Everything happens for a reason. Finding those reasons can make you. While these things were happening to me, I thought I was breaking, but in the end, the bad became the good. Sometimes in life, bad things happen that we have no control over, but that doesn't mean they shape us into something bad; it's supposed to happen so it can shape us into something good.

Betrayal

I was always such a happy girl
In my happy little world
Protected by dark knights and fire-breathing dragons
Until you poured reality into my fairy tale

I always had strength
Always carried the strongest weight
Won all the fights
Until you showed me your muscles

I always stood tall and confident
You stole that from me
I didn't understand why you chose to hurt me
Or how you could destroy a child's innocence

The feeling on the inside was a weight
I didn't think I could carry
It was a burst of flames
It was a gunshot wound
It was a shattered life

You pushed me down
When you knew I couldn't bear it any longer
I couldn't stand
I couldn't speak
I never stumbled so hard

My thoughts had me paralyzed
I thought I could trust you
I thought it was OK
I thought it was normal
Then I thought it was my fault

You chewed me up and spat me out
You tore my innocence into a million pieces
You set me on fire
And watched me burn

I'll never forget what you did to me
You will watch me grow
And you will feel nothing
But the weight of the shame you have given to me

I will not punish you
Every time you see my face guilt will eat you alive
For all that you have done to me
For all that you have put me through

You pushed me down
When you knew I couldn't bear it any longer
I couldn't stand
I couldn't speak
I never stumbled so hard

Forgiveness from someone
But never from me

Little Teenaged Girl

Little girl at the age of nine
Loses the war between God and her father
She held on as long as she could
But He was gone for good

Little girl at the age of ten
Begins to cry
She misses the days and the smiles
Her heart told her to never let go
But it just hurt too much

Little girl at the age of eleven
Overwhelming feelings for her broken family
She missed the silence and the whispers
She covers her ears
But the screams are too loud

Little girl at the age of twelve
Battlegrounds and constant anxiety
She loses her brother to suicidal thoughts
She holds the pieces of her heart
But it shatters everywhere

Teenaged girl at the age of thirteen
Baggage heavy and full
Hurting and losing control
She scratches her skin
But it's only a temporary fix

Teenaged girl at the age of fourteen
Undiscovered sicknesses
Alone and scared
She loses her mind
But she expected this

Teenaged girl at the age of fifteen
Diabetes struck her
Her heart began to sink
Too reckless to even bother
But it is all catching up

Teenaged girl at the age of sixteen
Suicide thoughts struck her mind
Is there a way out? Why am I thinking this way?
Her hands were held against her throat
But then it all went dark

Teenaged girl at the age of seventeen
She couldn't believe the journey she had been on
She never thought she'd leave the dark
She told her story
Someone was finally listening

Her

She spoke loudly
She cherished the bad
She pitied her sorrows
Even when she knew it made her sad

She was self-aware
Her mind was in not in control
Her heart was bashed in
And it all started to show

She hurt the people she loved
Even if it hurt her too
All she wanted was attention
But it only turned into aggression

In life we feel too much
We go through things we never understand
We manipulate our own minds
With the help of our own hands

I spent my whole life running and hiding from people
I didn't want to listen
To the emotional and mental abuse
But I did because I thought that's how you get respect

My mind had convinced me that I was nothing but bad
I thought I was in control

But it only made me mad
I was naïve
I was someone who I never thought I'd become

I became the victim in my own horror story
And the only person who was able to save me
Was *Her*

The Way Out

The feelings grew inside
like a plant
like an infection
and almost ended my life

The sounds of screams
voices broke
eyes focused
I was crippled and lost

Stuck in a cycle
back to back
spinning around
anxiety attacks

I had a pain with no way to explain
painted scars
scattered memories
it was all still the same

Saved letters and empty pill bottles
I hid in the shadows and lived in the dark
I was afraid I'd fall apart

I watched it all happen and take everything away from me
I burned the memories and all the notes
stepped on the ashes
and watched them fly away

I took a deep breath
and for the first time in a long time
death wasn't the only way out

I'm Sorry

Images

A child's memory only lasts for so long,
But hers
She could see from years before.
It all went by, and she almost lost everything.

She saw images playing in her head.
She felt energy she thought she'd never feel again.
The pressure grew stronger;
It became real.

She didn't understand,
And she didn't want to.
She just wanted to be safe again,
But she didn't know how to.

She was almost at the edge,
Feet above nothing,
About to let go—
She closed her eyes.

Her arms flew freely,
Heart beating through her chest,
Goosebumps over her arms—

For the moment,
She was free.

Times

The crack of dawn
My windows start to crack
The sun shines through my curtains
My alarm starts going off

Noon comes around
All I see is people
My chest starts to get numb
And I have nowhere to run

Evening skies
All colours mixed into one
The sun starts to hide
People rush to something and I rush to nothing

Lights turn off
It's dark outside
I see the moon and stars
I feel so alone

Midnight moon shines
A heavy wave of sadness overtakes me
I feel pressure and weakness
I don't know how I pulled myself together

But all I know is
I didn't want to die tonight

Knowing

Days and days
Become weeks and weeks
I am still sitting here
But not making a sound

I'm thinking and thinking
I'm losing my grip
What happened to me?
What am I becoming?

I stare at my reflection
And I start to cry
I pinch and hit myself
And start to wonder why

I start to feel every scar
And I listen closely
Why am I doing this to myself?
Why am I losing control?

The confident girl you saw
Isn't always seen
The positive girl you know
Isn't always shining

The lives that you see
Aren't always what they seem
You can look without seeing
And you could hear without knowing

Put yourself in their shoes
And see how many miles you could walk

Darkness

For about one second
I suddenly get distracted
My mind is skipping
And my pulse is racing

I start to fidget
Thoughts flood my mind
Am I nervous?
Or am I just afraid?

I start getting lost
And I appear in my bedroom
Crowded and suffocated
Sad and misunderstood

I start hyperventilating and shaking
I am stuck in the darkness
I am exhausted and afraid

I start to feel the pressure release
I am standing still
Awoken from a dream
But it wasn't a dream

For about one second
I lost my way, but I found the light
Out of darkness

Suffering

The clock is ticking
People are breathing
I am calm and smiling
But not for long

My thoughts are stuck
They don't seem to balance
They scramble and I lose control

The images in my head are fast-forwarding
They go to this place
To a place I don't want to be
And I break

My nerves are erupting
My chest collapses
My scars are torn
And I'm just sitting here watching

I black out
And my mind starts to spin
I can't suffer anymore
I need help

Feelings

Understanding
It is simple
It isn't hard
But it isn't easy

It starts with your ears
Then it makes its way around
Just like a virus
Until it has nowhere else to go

It enters your heart
It enters your mind
Then you start to feel it on the outside

It starts to form its own city
Limited space
Limited food
Limited time to stop it

Eventually it has to expand
It grows inside you
It attaches itself to you
It starts to feed off you

The only thing controlling it is
you

PART TWO

Inspirations

There are going to be things you go through and things you see that will change your life along with your perspective. I've seen so much in my life that opened my eyes to things I didn't think existed. The best thing I ever did for myself was to educate myself and learn to have compassion and empathy for others. You can find inspiration everywhere and anywhere if you give yourself time to see it and consume it. These inspirations are what really left a mark on my life, and I am truly grateful for these experiences.

Brother

The pain that lies in your eyes
The passion you have
The love you give
The intelligence you have inside
All break you down

You push me to be better
You yell till you can't breathe
You cry with a million emotions
And I always wonder why

You love so hard until it breaks you
You feel so much until it tears you apart
You suffer until you're down on the ground
And you never show us weakness

You taught me more than school
You showed me more than seeing
You stopped my tears from falling
You made me who I am

I'd be the world for you
I'd do it all to see you smile
I'd live as long as you wanted me to
You showed me more than anybody ever could

Friend

Having imagination
Dreaming big
Dressing beautifully
Shining bright and never broken

But living small
Seeing things differently
Insecurities are dimming your glow
And you are falling apart

Living in a world where things feel so wrong
Living in an environment where you
don't get to live every day
Having a voice so bold that it is silenced

Wandering around like you don't have a purpose
Invisible like you've never been around
Beaten like you don't have feelings
Taken for granted like you are nothing

You think you live in this world alone,
but I am right beside you
You feel invisible, but I can see you clearly
You think you're ugly, but all I see is beauty
You think you're silent, but all I hear is you

You are everything you're supposed to be and even more

Females

Little girl crying
Trying to see the good
Trying to understand life
Trying to believe in hope

Little girl smiling
She is only pretending
She is only nine
She is scared of everything
Including making it to ten

Teenage girl crying
Believes she is nothing
Believes she is fat and ugly
Believes no one loves her
Believes she won't make it

Young woman hiding
She hides her tears
She's ashamed of her scars
She embarrassed by her illness
Will the roller coaster ever end?

Woman crying
Growing up wasn't easy
Being alone is getting hard
Not loving is mental
Not knowing what's next is emotional

Old woman praying
She smiles because she forgives
She laughs because she is living
She loves because time is precious
She dies and now is forever at peace

Conflicted

Morning breeze hitting your face
The moment you awake
A sudden smile that has been painting itself for a while
Not everything is fake

Then suddenly
The wind feels like a storm
Your smile is washed away
And you are left with this pain

                              I don't know why I even try anymore

The storm has just begun
There is loud whistling and banging
The tunnels start to appear

                              I close my eyes

Tears running down my face
I breathe in and I hold
The storm will blow over soon
And so will negative thoughts of you

It's OK to be afraid
You are not alone

                              I breathe out

                  I open my eyes
And it was just another bump on a smooth beautiful road

Journey

In the beginning there are roads
Then you don't know which way to go
You stop and wonder
Then you hear the thunder
You're standing between crossroads
Unsure of which path to take
Breathing in the summer air
Wind blowing in your unwashed hair
You are wearing the same dress from decades ago
Your feelings grow stronger but you get weaker
The night sky falls
You are freezing and wheezing
The autumn leaves are coming
Then you start stumbling with nowhere else to go
The whistle in the wind blows
Your eyes and your heart follow the noise
The stoplights catch your attention
You wonder what the world would be like
If you only took a different path
You wish to turn back time
Deep breath in and open your eyes
In the beginning there are bumpy roads
You know which way to go
You never stop but always wonder
Then you hear the familiar thunder
But just to leave it all behind

Mirrors

A glass reflection
Of an object or a person
Close
And far

The objects I don't see
The feelings I do see
My reflection
I notice the most

The objects remind me of a scar
Or broken glass
The feelings spread like bacteria
And all I see is everything spinning
Like a carousel

I cannot handle the way I see my reflection
I don't know why I punish myself
It reminds me of a broken soul
Or hidden lie

It takes me down a road of memories I try to forget
I see and feel everything
I tackle myself
Like the running back of a rival team

Human

The reality of life hits you up
Society knocks you down
People speak loudly
But you're still standing proudly

No one understands the meaning
The meaning of the pain
Of the struggles
Of the tears and the blame

You have a look in your eyes
You have a look in your smile
It makes you no different
But all they see is different

You attempt to reach out
You decide to seek help
You'd do anything for a nibble
But all they do is knock you down

Sleeping in boxes
And sometimes a bench
Couch to couch
Struggling with the mess

Wearing the same sweater and jeans
Everyone is asking why you're never clean

You smile deep down inside
You're not where you want to be

You never let the looks and the judgments win
Because they don't know where you've been
You're screaming on the inside
But trying to make it on the outside

You watch society
You watch them throw away their lives
You watch ungrateful people
And you never understand why

You wonder about the chances and about the warmth
You wonder about those lives, but mostly yours

You seek attention
Just enough to get by
But little do they know
You're the strongest and the wisest alive

You're at your lowest point
But your spirit is awake
You're at your highest level
Even when you're about to break

But no one understands
And there's judgment at its finest
You watch us and all we do is watch you

Our People

Step by step dancing through the wind of the Aboriginals,
She held her head high, mumbling to
the beat of the hand drum.
The sound of the bells is the key to the song.
Her slippers slip through the grass of
the Eskasoni powwow grounds,
Then she knows she is home.

The sun is shining through her braids and feather earrings.
Her arms moving and her legs stomping,
She dances in circles while holding an Eagle's feather,
Then she knows what she is doing.

The hand drum is the beat of the soul;
The Eagle is the guide through our path.
We unite as a team of speakers
As we mumble but never stumble:
We are our people.

The old man who believes in his culture gets punished;
He says what he believes and how others do us wrong.
The ringing in his ears are voices
telling him that he is wrong;
They tell him he is wrong for speaking for us, but
We have the right to be us.

The skies are gray with sadness in our way.
He struggles to get his way because his way is right.
He shares his experiences with the
people who will protect him,
The people waving their hands but not just any hands,
Mi'kmaq hands.
We know we do right;
We know they do wrong.
The people who doubt us don't know
what we know because

The hand drum is the beat of the soul,
The Eagle is the guide through our path.
We unite as a team of speakers
As we mumble but never stumble.
We are our people,
And our people are us.

Don't stop what you believe in
When they stop taking away what they don't know—
That's when our culture will get stronger,
Because we are our people.

Warriors

You walked around for years
Proud of the choices you've made
Proud of the language you've had
Even proud of the creator you've worshipped

You took a group of people
Not just any people
First Nation people
And you broke them down
You sent one here and twenty-two there

You didn't take the time to understand
You took away their identity
You took them away from their lives
You took away everything that meant something to them
And buried it in the ground

You watched them suffer
And to this day they suffer
But all you do is laugh

You punished the child out of them
You punished the language out of them
And you killed the person inside them

You made something so sacred to them vanish
Vanish like happiness, the families, and the love

But they all kept in their essence in their hearts
They are called First Nations warriors
Warriors because of the fight
Because of the pain
And because they are strong

Some are still angry
Most are still hurting
Some found faith and forgiveness within themselves

We all know the stories that lie behind their eyes
We are all aware of the hurt and pain
That you have caused

We don't understand how someone can be so evil
But we understand that we have each other
Standing side by side
United as a team of WARRIORS

Reminder

Just a normal day just like the others
Weather change
Smiles and no worries
Passions and no distractions

You were delivered a sentence
That sentence changes you
All the sounds in the world get louder
And everything starts to get heavy

You freeze and forget everything
But in that moment
Suddenly everything is real
The pain is unbearable

The outside scar is a reminder
The inside scar is a constant reminder
The pain lasts forever
The tears seem endless and the questioning never stops

But the hurt does heal
The pain does stop
Then you are back to reality
And reminded to smile

There are moments when you realize
That it wasn't all for nothing and time was never wasted
Because there is always a reason

No Goodbyes

Dark clouds form
Tears make their way down my cheeks
Screams and memories
Are all stuck in my head

I was a nothing
Stuck in my own prison
Not recognizing myself
The earth told me stories and gave me redemption

A light had formed and dried up all my tears
The screams became a voice
And all I heard was wisdom

My light grew stronger and the dark clouds blew away
We all have a label
That is going to stay

As the years passed by
We were remade of steel
Our hearts had feelings and our brains felt real

We were brought down by others
We were told we didn't have the right to dream
We got the looks and the whispers
But we tried our best not to believe

No one understands our story
And what it took to get this far
We were taught more than we knew
With knowledge that will go only so far

Our experiences changed our lives
With love and hope no one can take away
We were made to believe that we can
And that's what we did

Belief

As she stands there
Constantly pulling her skin
She realizes what she is doing
Now the thoughts in her head start to win

As she stands there
Paranoid from a whisper
Nervous from all the stares
She punishes herself again

As she sits there
In disgust
She feels horrible
She scars herself once more

As she lies there
She cries and wonders why
She's damaged and afraid
She's weak and tired

As she screams for help
She gets what she deserves
But yet she wonders how

As she stands there able to stand
She cried out "Thank you!" because she believed
There was a bigger plan

PART THREE

Finding Myself

Everything I've been through was part of a journey. I have discovered many things about myself. I have realized a lot of the wrong that happened wasn't right. I have thought about my life and my experiences so many times. I was inspired and seen. In using my voice and in finally being heard, I was finally able to breathe, despite all those times when I felt as though I was drowning. It has often been so dark on this journey, and I felt stuck underneath barbed wire. I realized that the only way to turn on the light was to do something about it, to work through all the pain and finally bring myself out of darkness. If you wait and wait for someone to save you, you will never be saved.

Be your own hero.

Beginnings

Words that I did not understand
Words that I did not care for
Words and words—just a blur

I wrote down things
I wrote down the stings
They all made a scar
But did they really?

The silence on the paper
The expression of nothing
The waste of power
Was all written in my word-form

What do I feel?
When will I heal?
How do I cope?
Where is the rope?

I get confused
Then I start to bruise
What have I done?
This isn't what I've become

I begin the journey of meaning
The journey of life and pain
I opened my eyes
And I discovered what it really means to me

My poems became powerful
My words became expressive
My writing became emotions
My story became progressive

My life is in my words
And my words are about my life

Disguise

Sitting in a white room
Listening to bickering
Drawing no attention
Letting go

I've been told once, twice
And even a hundred times
That I've got what it takes
That I've got to have faith

I was too young to understand
I was too young to care
Too young to be aware

The responsibilities lie in my hands
The sacrifices lie in my eyes
The bravery lies in my blood
The disguise lies in me

Blaming myself is no good
But harming myself isn't any good either

I open my eyes and begin to see
My hands and my hurt
My balance and my curse
I begin to see me

The clock was ticking and I caught it
My mind was blown but I caught it
My tears were endless but I caught them
I was falling but I caught myself

I see me
Even if I've been in disguise

Confident

Beauty lies on the inside
And always on the outside
Confidence grows into your heart
Then into your mind
Your energy starts to develop

Opening up is something we do
We open our minds
We open our visions
We open our hearts
Because these are the things we do

I look at my reflection
And I see more than I will ever see
I will notice everything that is wrong
And ignore all that is good

It's not worrying about what you look like
It's about seeing your reflection without having to look
Into the mirror
Or take a selfie

Your beauty is one of a kind
And your soul is your own flow
A reflection isn't only in a mirror
Or in a rain puddle in the ground
It is what you can see on the inside
And all I see is beauty

Tongue-Tied

My voice left
Because I was unsure
My voice left me here
And took all my words

As I walk these streets wondering
Holding my breath
Speechless and unfed
I try

I run to a group of people
And try to speak
They don't understand
They are laughing and I am crying

So I walk away ashamed
I let it get the best of me
And never try to speak again

You made me ashamed of who I was
Because I didn't speak like you
Because I wasn't a part of you
But I did look like you

The Fade

The warmth of my skin shatters
The pupils of my eyes expands
My hands begin to shake
And my temper starts to erupt

My pulse begins to fade
And my brain starts to speed up
The wind is heavy but soft
The rain is loud but focused

No one knows the difference
No one understands
No one hears the thoughts
No one gives a helping hand

I try to defend my beliefs
I try to protect my independence
I'm falling apart
And the storm is never-ending

Lightning strikes
And again it goes
All hope is lost
And I just start to explode

My thoughts are back
And they don't seem to break
My heart starts to twist
And my bones start to shake

I look up and see blue
The bluest of the sky
The darkness fades
And so does the shade

It builds up inside and releases
The pain, the sorrows
The humiliation, the shame
The disappointment, the sadness
Aches in a way

Every wound heals itself
The help of mercy brings light
That light meets you
And it takes a while for you to dim

Forgiveness

The sun is shining
The birds are chirping
The wind has movement
And here comes the storm

Out of the blue
Comes darkness
Darkness rolling towards me
I'm running but I'm plastered to the floor

I look forward and see light
I look back and see only dark
I'm running and running
But only in slow motion

My mind is saying *Keep going*
But my heart is screaming out forgiveness
I take a step back
And listen

Life shows you mercy
Life shows you light
Life shows you pain

I am reaching out
But getting pulled under
The past is the past
But why am I still stuck

I scream and I shout
I feel the burns, the scars
I feel the hurt
All pushing the darkness away

We all take challenges
And never realize we finished
My challenge was forgiveness
And I ran right past it

Finding My Way

As the days pass by
So do the months
And then the year

I'm stuck on repeat
Pen in my hand
Blank paper by my feet

What am I doing wrong?
I have a talent inside of me
I lost my touch
When will I find my way?

I'm losing my grip
I'm losing my control
I'm spinning around in circles
And no one even knows

I'm trying to find my way
I'm trying to find the time
I sit on the ground
And I am drowning

I get into my mind and I set my goals
I released many of the stresses
And started to let go

I believed in myself
And I believed in relief
Now look at me
I am a non-stop writing machine

Calling

I hear the wind calling out my name:
The whisper is so soft.
My life is on pause for just two seconds.

For two seconds I lose control.
All my thoughts break free,
And my body starts to let go.

I am far from the worst,
But I feel my disguise,
My pain,
My anxiety –
I'm two ticks from going insane.

I believe in myself,
And I believe in this world,
But my thoughts confuse me deeply,
And I am only letting go.

My life was on pause for just two seconds:
I could hear the wind;
I could feel the storm.

I hear a calling from my dreams,
Calling out for me.

I Am the Reason

As I lie beneath my ceiling
Smothered by these walls
Secured by the floor
I begin to wonder and I never stop

I draw attention to my mind
I draw attention to the blinds
I draw attention to the noise
I draw attention to letting go

I wrote words
Words in pen
Words in marker
Words in my mind

I wrote the words of wisdom
That I had all this time
I was afraid when I started
And now I am free

All the ideas scatter around the room
All the stories I've painted splash onto the walls
All the pains that were written before I fall

I am the reason for that creation
I am reason for it all
I let all my doubts wash away because I know
I am the light that will shine very bright

Making it

I've been pushed around
Ruined for something else
Ashamed of what has happened
With no one else to blame

I wonder what's inside
Inside of me
Is what I need to see

I've been told I'm no good
I've been shamed for whatever they could
I sit there in silence
But I know I will make it

I close my eyes
And a motion picture starts to form
My life is in motion
But in my own word-form

I open my eyes
And suddenly express
My life is a tragedy
But now is the best

I still wonder
I still hear the screams
I still feel the scars

It's all drilled into my memory
A word will define that memory
The memories that I've had
The past that was pained
I know that someday it will make me less ashamed

And that is when I will know that I've made it

Afterword

A writer's words have many different meanings, more than any dictionary will ever have. Don't be afraid to put yourself out there. Being afraid stops us from enjoying many things in life. I believe that if your dreams don't scare you, then they aren't dreams.

You have to be willing to work hard and to allow yourself to write what you desire. Allow yourself to write badly. Allow yourself to be criticized. And most importantly, allow yourself to breathe. It's OK to overthink everything you do. I did. But I was overwhelmed because all I ever wanted from life was to be published. I was told by someone I very much looked up to that I was never going to make it as a writer. That hurt me, but I wasn't allowing myself to be criticized—I was allowing that person to shatter my dreams.

No one can take your dreams away from you unless you let them. I wrote for years and years before someone finally noticed me, and that changed my life forever. I wouldn't have known what I had inside me if it weren't for that little push.

I want to inspire people to tell their stories, to paint their scars, to scream out their passion, because I know how dark it gets inside sometimes. Writing has allowed me to express myself any way I want. Writing my poems saved my life because I painted a picture of all my tragedies and pain just to get to this point in life. Everything is meant to happen for a reason.

Be patient.

Be strong.

Be spontaneous.

Be brave

And be you!

Writing and Drawing Prompts

Write or draw about your culture …

Write or draw about a struggle …

Write or draw about your passion ...

Write or draw how you feel right now ...

Write or draw about something that is important to you …

Write or draw about what loyalty, strength, and bravery mean to you ...

Write or draw about someone you love …

Write or draw about your goals and dreams …

Printed in the United States
by Baker & Taylor Publisher Services